JUN 2008

HEALTHY CHOICES

HEALTHY EATING

Cath Senker

PowerKiDS
press.

New York

Text copyright © Cath Senker 2004
The right of Cath Senker to be identified as the author of this Work has
been asserted by her in accordance with the Copyright, Designs, and Patents Act 1988

Published in 2008 by The Rosen Publishing Group, Inc.
29 East 21st Street, New York, NY 10010

First Edition

Consultant: Jayne Wright
Design: Sarah Borny

The publishers would like to thank the following for allowing
us to reproduce their pictures in this book:
Corbis; 20 / Hodder Wayland Picture Library; 5, 6, 7, 8, 9, 10
11, 12, 13, 14, 15, 17, 18, 19, 21 / Zul Mukhida; 4, 16

Library of Congress Cataloging-in-Publication Data

Senker, Cath.
  Healthy eating / Cath Senker. — 1st ed.
     p. cm. — (Healthy choices)
  Includes index.
  ISBN 978-1-4042-4303-3 (library binding)
  1. Nutrition—Juvenile literature. 2. Health—Juvenile literature. 3. Children—
Nutrition—Juvenile literature. I. Title.
  RA784.S464 2008
  613.2—dc22
                                    2007032805

Manufactured in China

Contents

What foods should I eat?

Your body needs a balance of different kinds of foods to grow and be healthy. There are five main food groups.

1. Bread, potatoes, breakfast cereals, and other cereals, such as pasta, corn, rice, and oats. Also beans and *pulses*

2. Fruit and vegetables

3. Milk and *dairy foods*

4. Meat, fish, and alternatives, such as beans and pulses, nuts, and eggs

5. Foods with fat and sugar, such as cookies, cake, butter, jelly, and ice cream

Which food groups can you see here?

(Answer on page 23)

Foods from the first group should be the main part of your **diet**. Fill yourself up with cereals. Eat plenty of crispy, crunchy fruit and vegetables, too. Your body needs less dairy foods and meat.

It's fine to eat foods such as french fries and cake now and then. Be careful not to fill up on them, though. It's fun to try different foods from all the food groups.

What foods give you energy?

Foods such as bread, breakfast cereals, potatoes, pasta, and rice give you energy that lasts. When you are playing sports, these will keep you going until the end of the game.

Whole wheat bread and *whole grain* rice and pasta are better for you than the white kinds. They're tasty, too.

A baked potato with cheese makes a delicious energy food.

What do you spread on your bread? Be careful not to use too much butter or margarine.

The way we

prepare energy food is

important. Try not to eat

fried food, such as french fries,

too often.

Do you ever get hungry between meals? Pack a healthy

snack. Have an apple, a banana, or some raisins.

Why are fruits and vegetables healthy?

Fruits and vegetables give you *vitamins*. Vitamins help your body to work properly and fight *infection*.

There are many kinds of vegetables to choose from. Have you tried snow peas or zucchini? You can eat some vegetables raw. Others have to be cooked.

Fruit is fantastic. Do you enjoy juicy pears and crunchy apples? Oranges are delicious and sweet.

Have you tried melon,

peaches, plums, and grapes?

Remember that fruit juice is good for you, too.

Do you eat at least five kinds of fruits and vegetables every day? That's what your body needs.

Do I have to drink milk?

It's good to drink milk. Milk and **dairy** foods, such as cheese and yogurt, help you to grow. They make your bones and teeth strong and healthy.

For breakfast, enjoy a big bowl of breakfast cereal with milk. It gives you lots of energy. Go for cereal sweetened with fruit instead of sugar.

Yogurt is a tasty, healthy snack. Which flavors have you tried?

Cheese and yogurt are good for you, too. Children's yogurts sometimes have a lot of added sugar, though. Check the *ingredients* on a pot of yogurt. Does it have sugar in it? Try making your own fruit yogurt. Add your favorite fruit to natural yogurt. It's healthier without added sugar.

Are meat and fish good for me?

Meat and fish are *protein* foods. They help you to grow and stay healthy. Protein foods have vitamins, too.

Meat is a great way to get protein. You need to be careful, though. Some meaty foods, such as sausages and bacon, are full of fat. Eat them only occasionally. Chicken and *lean* meat are better for you.

Fish makes a tasty dish. Try some different kinds.

Oily fish, such as

mackerel and

sardines, are

very good

for you.

Fish is

better

without batter.

Fried fish is fatty.

It's better not to have fish sticks too often.

Why can't I eat candies every day?

Think of all your favorite party foods. Are some of them on these lists?

Sugary foods:

sodas and colas, candies,

jelly, puddings,

cake, cookies

Fatty foods:

chocolate, french fries,

cake, cookies, ice cream,

butter, cream

It's fine to eat these things at a party, because you don't go to parties every day.

Eating fatty and sugary foods every day would be bad for you. Many of these foods have lots of salt, too. Too much fat and salt are bad for your heart. Sugar can rot your beautiful teeth.

It's sensible to eat just a few sweet treats, now and then.

What's wrong with sodas and colas?

Most soft drinks are full of sugar. We all know sugar is bad for our teeth.

It's OK to have a soda with your meal once in a while. If you drink sugary drinks between meals, though, the sugar stays on your teeth. It can lead to **tooth decay**.

How many times do you brush your teeth each day? You should brush them twice a day.

When you're thirsty, pour yourself some fresh water.

Mix water with different kinds of fruit juice for a change.

Milk is healthy, too. Why not make a milkshake?

What if I'm a vegetarian?

Everyone needs to eat protein. You can get protein from plenty of foods, not just meat and fish. **Vegetarians** need to choose several of these delicious foods as part of a balanced diet. Then they will have no problem getting enough protein.

Enjoy a boiled egg or try some *tofu*. Go nutty for nuts and tasty seeds. Stir them into pasta or put them on pizzas.

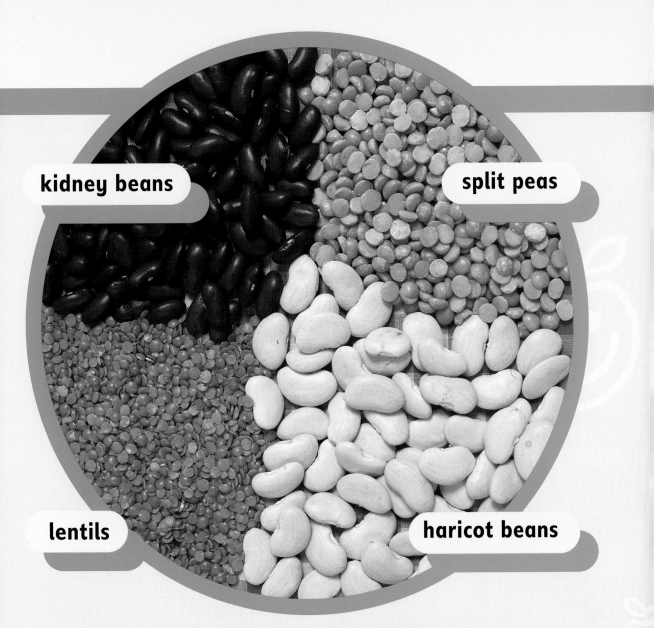

kidney beans

split peas

lentils

haricot beans

Be full of beans—and other *pulses*. Pulses are the seeds of vegetable plants. They come in all shapes, sizes, and colors. You'll find them in soups and salads, pies, and curries.

What are special diets?

Some people can't eat certain foods, because they make them feel very sick. You might know someone who is **allergic** to nuts.

Other people avoid certain foods because of their beliefs. Muslims and Jewish people don't eat meat from a pig. Hindus will not eat beef. Vegetarians do not eat meat or fish, because they don't want to harm animals.

This Jewish boy is enjoying a pita bread snack that contains no meat from a pig.

Everyone has some foods they really love and others they really hate. You need a balance of lots of different kinds of food to stay healthy. Make sure you enjoy your food!

Glossary and index

allergic 20   Having an allergy. It means you get sick when you eat a certain food.

dairy foods 4, 10   Foods that are made from milk.

diet 5   The foods and drinks that you usually have.

infection 8   An illness that affects a part of your body, such as an ear infection.

ingredients 11   The things that a food is made of.

lean meat 12   Meat with little or no fat in it.

oily fish 13   Fish that has oils that you need for good health.

protein 12   A natural substance in meat, eggs, fish, and some other foods. People need protein to grow and stay healthy.

pulses 4, 19   The seeds of some vegetable plants that are eaten as food, such as peas and lentils.

tofu 18   A soft, white food made from soybeans. It looks a little bit like cheese.

tooth decay   16   When a tooth begins to rot, leaving a hole that needs to be filled.

vegetarians   18   People who do not eat meat or fish.

vitamins   8   Natural substances found in different foods. They help people to grow and stay healthy.

whole grain   6   Made with all the grain of a cereal, with nothing taken out.

whole wheat   6   Made with whole grains of wheat.

Answer to question:

P.4   The food groups in the picture are from groups 1, 2, and 4.

Finding out more

Books to read:

A First Look at Health and Fitness
by Pat Thomas (Barron's Educational, 2001)

Eat Well (Safe and Sound)
by Angela Royston (Heinemann Library, 1999)

My Food Pyramid
(DK Children, 2007)

Showdown at the Food Pyramid
by Rex Barron (Putnam Juvenile, 2004)

Why Should I Eat Well?
by Claire Llewellyn and Mike Gordon (Barron's Educational, 2005)

Web Sites
Due to the changing nature of Internet links, PowerKids Press has developed an online list of Web sites related to the subject of this book. This site is regularly updated. Please use this link to access this list:
www.powerkidslinks.com/health/eating